GETTING TO KNOW THE WORLD'S GREATEST ARTISTS

D I E G O
RIVERA

WRITTEN AND ILLUSTRATED BY MIKE VENEZIA

CONSULTANT MEG MOSS

CHILDRENS PRESS®
CHICAGO

To the kids at St. Pius X School.

Cover: *Birth of Class Consciousness*, by Diego Rivera. 1926-27.
Fresco. Chapel, Universidad Autonoma de Chapingo, Mexico.
Photograph © Dirk Bakker.

Project Editor: Shari Joffe
Photo researcher: Jan Izzo

Library of Congress-in-Publication Data

Venezia, Mike
    Diego Rivera / written and illustrated by Mike Venezia.
        p.   cm. -- (Getting to know the world's greatest artists)
    ISBN 0-516-02299-7
    1. Rivera, Diego, 1886-1957--Juvenile literature. 2. Artists-
    Mexico--Biography--Juvenile literature.   [1. Rivera, Diego,
    1886-1957 2. Artists 3. Painting, Mexican.   4. Painting, Modern-
    -Mexico.   5. Art appreciation .]   I. Rivera, Diego, 1886-1957.
    II. Title. III. Series: Venezia, Mike. Getting to know the world's
    greatest artists.
    N6559.R58V45   1994
    759. 972--dc20
    [B]   94-11650
                                                                    CIP
                                                                     AC

Self Portrait,
by Diego Rivera.
1941. Oil on canvas,
24 x 16 $\frac{7}{8}$ inches.
Smith College
Museum of Art,
Northampton,
Massachusetts.
Gift of Irene Rich
Clifford, 1977.

Diego Rivera thought it was important to make paintings for everyday working people to enjoy. He hoped his art would teach people about their past and give them hope for the future.

The Totonac Civilization, by Diego Rivera. 1950.
Fresco, 16 $^1/_{10}$ x 17 $^2/_{10}$ feet. Palacio Nacional,
Mexico City, Mexico. Photograph © Dirk Bakker.

To make it easier for lots of people
to see his artwork, Diego Rivera
painted huge pictures called *murals*
on the walls of schools, churches,
hospitals, hotels, and government
buildings. Diego usually painted on
wet plaster with watercolors, a
technique known as fresco painting.

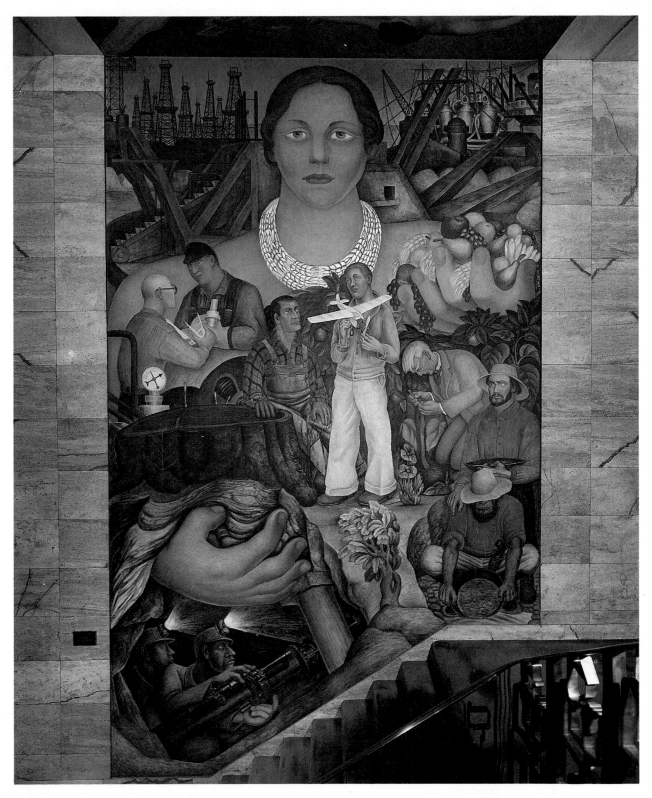

Allegory of California, by Diego Rivera. Fresco,
471.69 square feet. Pacific Stock Exchange,
San Francisco, California. Photograph © Dirk Bakker.

Diego was a great storyteller. His paintings usually tell a story about the history of Mexico, or people at work, or how something is made. In *The Making of a Fresco*, Diego showed himself and his assistants painting a mural. He also showed sculptors, and engineers and architects planning new buildings. Some people became upset when they saw that Diego had painted himself with his backside to them. They thought he was being rude. Diego Rivera often upset people with his work.

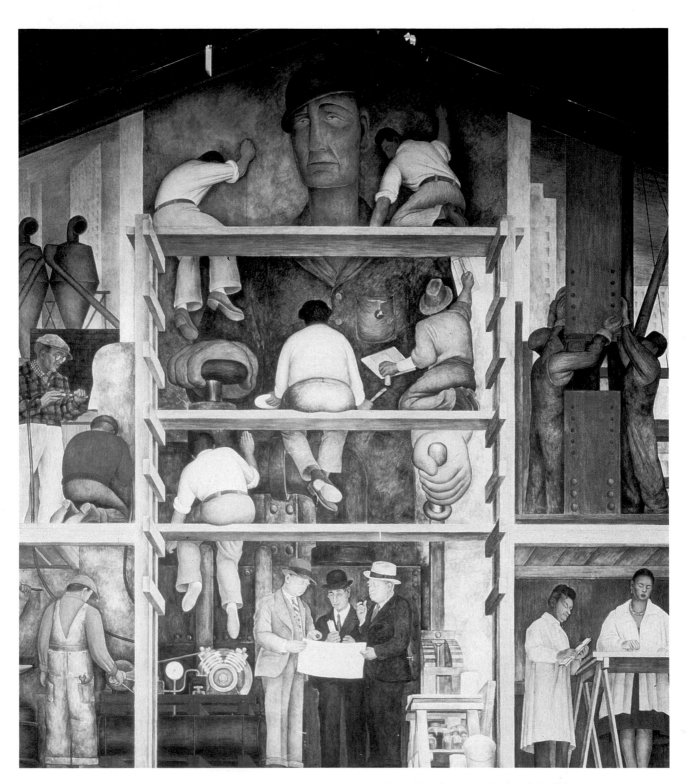

The Making of a Fresco Showing the Building of a City, by Diego
Rivera. April-June, 1931. Fresco, 22 feet 7 inches x 29 feet 9 inches.
San Francisco Art Institute. Photograph © David Wakely.

Diego Rivera as
a child. Courtesy
of The Detroit
Institute of Arts.

Diego Rivera was born in 1886 in
the Mexican town of Guanajuato. He
always had a wonderful imagination.
When he was very young, he spent
lots of time in the Mexican forest with
his pet goat. He said he made friends
with all the animals there, even the
dangerous and poisonous ones.

When he was a little older, Diego
started to draw. He particularly loved
to draw inventions that he made up
in his head, and the mechanical parts
of toys he took apart. Diego drew on

anything he could find—even the walls! This became such a problem that his father decided to cover a whole room for him with canvas in order to save the rest of the house.

When he was ten years old, Diego decided he wanted to become an artist. Because he was an excellent student (and very stubborn once he made up his mind), his parents sent him to the famous San Carlos art academy in Mexico City. Diego's teachers taught him to draw and paint. They also taught him all the important things they had learned from the great artists of Spain, France, and Italy.

Satire on the comet that appeared in 1899.
Reproduced from *Posada's Popular Mexican Prints*, published by Dover Publications, Inc.

Diego said he learned about the art of his own country from a teacher he found all by himself. José Posada owned a small printing shop near the academy. Diego would often stop by to watch Posada make his drawings and prints.

Diego had never seen anything like Posada's pictures of Mexican legends and everyday events. He thought Posada's drawings were so full of energy and life that they might jump off the page at any moment.

The Grinder, by Diego Rivera. 1924.
Encaustic on canvas, 35 $^4/_{10}$ x 46 inches.
Museo de Arte Moderno, Mexico City, Mexico.
Photograph © Dirk Bakker.

Years later, Diego too would
paint scenes of everyday events.

Woman at the Well, by Diego Rivera. 1913. Oil on canvas, 56 $^6/_{10}$ x 52 $^3/_{10}$ inches. Museo Nacional de Arte, Mexico City, Mexico. Photograph © Dirk Bakker.

While Diego was growing up, Mexico's government wasn't working very well. Few people in Mexico had enough money to be able to enjoy themselves, and hardly anyone knew how to read. Diego saw that many people in Mexico were living almost like slaves. It bothered him very much.

In 1907, when Diego was twenty, he went to study art in Europe. There he became friends with artists who were already famous, like Pablo Picasso and Amedeo Modigliani. Diego was influenced by these artists. Soon, he started to become known for his own paintings. Some of them looked very much like Pablo Picasso's cubist paintings.

Untitled (Man with a Mustache, Buttoned Vest and Pipe, Seated in an Armchair), by Pablo Picasso. 1915. Oil on canvas, 51 ^{2}/$_{10}$ x 35 ^{2}/$_{10}$ inches. Gift of Mrs. Leigh B. Block in memory of Albert D. Lasker, 1952.1116. Photograph © 1994, The Art Institute of Chicago. All rights reserved.

Even though Diego Rivera was doing well in Europe, he felt that something was missing from his art. Diego worried that his paintings were being enjoyed only by well-educated people who were wealthy enough to buy them for their homes. He thought that art should be enjoyed by everyone—especially poor, working people.

While on a trip to Italy, Diego saw frescoes that had been painted hundreds of years earlier.

Flight into Egypt,
by Giotto. Fresco,
72 8/10 x 78 7/10
inches. Scrovegni
Chapel, Padua,
Italy. Scala/Art
Resource, NY.

Usually, these were painted on the
walls of churches (like the one above),
so everyone in a town or city could
enjoy them. Diego decided he would
return to Mexico to make paintings for
all the people there to enjoy.

When Diego arrived in Mexico, he was asked to paint a large mural for an important school. Diego named the painting *Creation*.

People all over Mexico thought it was wonderful! They loved the beautiful, rich colors; the strong, solid shapes of the people; and the skillful way Diego had made the painting fit into the space of the building.

Creation, by Diego Rivera. 1922-23. Fresco, encaustic and gold leaf, 23 2/10 x 39 3/10 feet. Escuela Nacional Preparatoria, Anfiteatro Bolivar, Mexico City, Mexico. Photograph © Dirk Bakker.

Diego was soon given more jobs. He worked hard to get away from his European influences and create a style of art that was all his own. He especially wanted to make art that was more Mexican in feeling. Other artists also began painting murals at this time. David Siqueiros and José

22

Clemente Orozco were two other Mexican artists who became famous for their beautiful and powerful works. It seemed like murals were popping up all over Mexico.

Diego often painted revolutionary events and the leaders who were fighting to change things in Mexico so people would have more rights and freedom. Some people, though,

thought things in Mexico were just fine
the way they were. They sometimes
became angry at what the mural artists
were showing, and would throw rocks
at the artists and their work! Diego
decided to arm himself for protection.

During the 1930s, Diego Rivera was invited to paint murals in the United States. One of the most famous was called *Detroit Industry*. Diego painted it on the walls of a large room in the art museum in Detroit, Michigan.

Detroit Industry, South Wall, by Diego Rivera. 1932-33. Mural. © The Detroit Institute of Arts, Founders Society Purchase, Edsel B. Ford Fund and Gift of Edsel B. Ford.

In one section of *Detroit Industry*, Diego showed factory workers making steel and engine parts for cars. Diego saw beauty in modern machinery as well as in people. He gave his mural lots of life by making

Detroit Industry, North Wall, 1932-33. Mural.
© The Detroit Institute of Arts, Founders Society Purchase,
Edsel B. Ford Fund and Gift of Edsel B. Ford.

a conveyor belt move through the huge
factory almost like a snake. Fire from
the open furnace and the giant machines
remind some people of Indian gods at
an ancient Mexican ceremony.

Diego Rivera lived to be seventy-one years old, and had a very exciting life. He and his wife, Frida Kahlo, who was also a famous artist, attracted attention wherever they went.

Diego Rivera working on a mural in 1950.
Courtesy of The Detroit Institute of Arts.

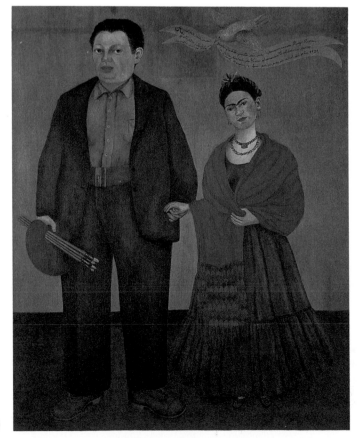

Sometimes people didn't like what Diego showed in his paintings. One of Diego's murals in the United States was torn off the

Frida and Diego Rivera, by Frida Kahlo. 1931. Oil on canvas, 39 3/8 x 31 inches. San Francisco Museum of Modern Art, San Francisco, California. Albert M. Bender Collection, Gift of Albert M. Bender.

wall after Diego insisted on showing a portrait of a Russian revolutionary leader who was unpopular in America at the time.

Diego always painted what he felt was important, no matter what anyone thought.

Detail of *Man, Controller of the Universe*, by Diego Rivera. 1934. Fresco, 15 $^9/_{10}$ x 37 $^6/_{10}$ feet. Museo de Palacio de Bellas Artes, Mexico City, Mexico City. Photograph © Dirk Bakker.

It was especially important to him to show the history and beauty of the Mexican people he loved so much.

Flower Day, by Diego Rivera. 1925. Oil on canvas, 58 x 47 $^1/_2$ inches. Los Angeles County Museum of Art, Los Angeles County Funds.

The History of Medicine in Mexico: The People's Demand for Better Health, by Diego Rivera. 1953. Hospital de la Raza, Mexico City, Mexico. Photograph © Dirk Bakker.

Most of Diego Rivera's murals are in Mexico, but a few are in the United States. If you get a chance to see one, you'll notice how well it fits into the design of the building. Diego thought a lot about the architecture of a building before starting to paint.

The works of art in this book came from:
The Art Institute of Chicago
Escuela Nacional Preparatoria Anfiteatro Bolivar, Mexico City, Mexico
Founders Society Detroit Institute of Art, Detroit, Michigan
Hospital de la Raza, Mexico City, Mexico
Los Angeles County Museum of Art, Los Angeles, California
Museo de Arte Moderno, Mexico City, Mexico
Museo de Palacio de Bellas Artes, Mexico City, Mexico
Museo Nacional de Arte, Mexico City, Mexico
The Museum of Modern Art, New York, New York
Pacific Stock Exchange, San Francisco, California
Palacio Nacional, Mexico City, Mexico
San Francisco Art Institute, San Francisco, California
San Francisco Museum of Modern Art, San Francisco, California
Smith College Museum of Art, Northampton, Massachusetts
Scrovegni Chapel, Padua, Italy
Universidad Autonoma de Chapingo, Chapingo, Mexico